HOW TO BUY
PROPERTY IN
BULGAR

GW00659269

A BRIT'S SCRAPBOOK

HOW TO BUY PROPERTY IN BULGARIA

JOANNA LOSACK

LEANMARKETING™
★PRESS★

First Published In Great Britain 2005
by Lean Marketing Press
www.BookShaker.com

ISBN 0 9545681 3 3

Typeset in Garamond

ACKNOWLEDGEMENTS

I would like to extend my thanks to Nick Parkin and his team at Bulgarian Apartments and Adventures in Veliko Tarnovo, (*www.bg–aa.com*) for their support in buying my rural properties. Also Stephane Lambert and Andy Anderson of Stara Planina Properties (*www.stara–planina.com*) for all their help and advice in writing this book along with Sebastian Kinsman of Balkan Ski Chalets for continued help in buying my apartment in Bansko. My thanks also to Nicola Cairncross (*www.nicolacairncross.com*) for writing the forward to this book.

Finally thanks to my editor, Joe Gregory, for turning my initial manuscript into a polished final product and Debbie Jenkins at Lean Marketing Press and BookShaker.com for her decisive marketing advice and abundance of good ideas.

Most of all – I thank my two boys, Johnny (12) and Sam (8). Without their patience, support and pocket money – I would never have been able to start my Bulgarian Adventure!

Joanna Losack

CONTENTS

FOREWORD

As a Wealth Coach, I spend a lot of time with my clients working on Property Investment, one of the "Four Lanes of the Wealth Highway" and buying property overseas is always an extremely popular part of those discussions.

For many of us, buying a holiday home or investment property overseas is the ultimate dream, one that we will fulfil when we really make it and "succeed". Well, Joanna Losack's excellent book will bring that dream so much closer for many people, as she comprehensively shares the details we would all need, in order to be able to successfully buy in the beautiful, but little known country of Bulgaria. Property is incredibly affordable there – with prices being comparable to Spain in the 1960's and France in the 1980's.

As a committed Greekophile, even I found my heart racing with excitement as she describes the country, the people and the excellent investment opportunities available – Joanna obviously has a great love of Bulgaria, the land and its people.

The book contains a wealth of useful contacts, websites, checklists and worksheets to help you hone your investment or holiday home buying strategy. I wouldn't consider beginning a search for a property of any kind in Bulgaria without buying this book immediately. And I wouldn't now consider buying a property abroad without seriously considering Bulgaria.

Nicola Cairncross, Wealth Coach,
www.nicolacairncross.com, December 2004

WHY INVEST IN BULGARIA?

"Bulgaria Is The Fastest Developing Tourist Destination In Europe"
– SOFIA MORNING NEWS, MAR 2004

Why Bulgaria? Because the scenery is stunning and the climate is wonderful. Because the people are friendly and the taxes are fair. Because there are numerous historic towns and unchanged rural traditions. Because the cost of living is low, food tastes like it really should and the property prices are exceedingly low.

Where else could you buy a 'rural retreat' for just £3000?

Whether a property is being bought for investment, a second home or holiday home, or a retirement home, prices are low but are set to rise. This increase will be fuelled by the continued growth in tourism with the increasing realisation that Bulgaria is an acceptable alternative to say Spain, Portugal or Greece as a holiday destination.

VALUE FOR MONEY

Properties in Bulgaria offer excellent value for money compared to other holiday destinations in Europe. They also offer a good investment considering the long–term prospects for the country. An average seaside villa, or a three bedroom chalet in one of Bulgaria's ski resorts can be purchased for around £40,000. While there are properties priced even lower than this, one should consider that they are likely to require some renovation work. Property prices in the more rural locations, especially around Veliko Turnovo, the old medieval capital, are exceptionally low.

WHAT WAS POSSIBLE IN 2004...
3 bed House £8,432
11 Bed House £45,500
**I bought my first house in May 2004 for £3,500
it's now (Nov 2004) worth nearly £10,000!**

LONG DEPENDABLE SUMMERS – CRISP WHITE WINTERS

Bulgaria's weather is just one of the reasons why tourist figures have risen so sharply over the last two years. Bulgaria offers both a hot Mediterranean climate as well as skiing in the winter resorts. Generally summers are longer and warmer than in the UK (and guaranteed) while the winters are shorter but can be more severe. The Black Sea coast is less cold in the winter, than inland areas, and rarely sees snow. From May to September, average temperatures are 30 degrees Celsius and often above in the peak summer period.

HOW THE WEATHER MEASURES UP...

	London	Burgas	Madrid
Top Temperature	71.0 °F	80.0 °F	90.0 °F
Avg. Annual Temperature	61.4 °F	66.8 °F	69.0 °F
Annual Rainfall	29.7 inches	21.8 inches	17.8 inches

GET MORE FOR LESS

The cost of living in Bulgaria is another reason why visitors and property buyers are on the increase. Living costs are substantially lower than in other European countries and amongst the lowest worldwide.

Whatever your budget, Bulgaria offers considerably better value for money than other European holiday destinations, but things are changing fast. Since last year, prices have increased, on average, by 20% and this year there are even more substantial increases in certain sectors of the market.

Bulgaria is currently representing an excellent opportunity for investment, comparable to Spain 20–30 years ago. Each region has its own appeal, but Bulgaria, in essence, currently offers good value for money in a stable environment and is just three hours away by plane from the UK.

COST OF LIVING COMPARISON...		
	Britain	**Bulgaria**
Bottle of Red Wine	£5.00	£1.00
Pint of Lager	£2.50	30p
Packet of Cigarettes	£4.00	30p
Local Taxi Journey	£5.00	50p
3 Course Dinner for 2 (with wine)	£50.00	£7.00
Litre of Petrol	90p	50p
Brand New 4x4	£20,000	£6,000
Renault Clio	£9,000	£4,000

BRIT FRIENDLY – LOW CRIME

Street crime is rare, and crimes against people are statistically very low compared to Western Europe. Bulgaria is a peaceful, law abiding and trouble–free country. As elsewhere, it is sensible to take precautions, such as not carrying all your money in cash, showing off cash or expensive jewellery in the streets, and taking care of your belongings. Bulgarians are friendly and welcoming to foreigners.

 ## PRICE RISES LIKELY TO SLOW AFTER 2007

"Average 2003 increases 23–28% some areas increased 100% in 2003"
– SOFIA MORNING NEWS, FEB 2004

Prices are rising rapidly as Bulgaria's EU accession draws closer – experts predict that this rapid growth will tail off following this point. The best time to get bargain investments was yesterday, the next best time to buy is today!

IT'S PART OF THE EUROPEAN UNION... ALMOST...

Bulgaria joined NATO in 2004 and is striving towards proposed accession to the European Union in 2007. Between now and then, property prices are expected to rise substantially and then continue at a slightly slower pace, after EU membership has been granted.

FINDING A PROPERTY

"Low property prices, beautiful countryside, historic towns and unchanged rural traditions. The cost of living is also surprisingly low and makes Turkey look expensive. The food is good and a meal out costs £5, a beer 50p, and an espresso 15p"
– THE TIMES, FEB 2004

WHERE TO BUY, WHAT TO BUY

There are many areas to consider when buying property and it depends on whether you are a lover of the sea, a snow bunny, a mountain hiker or if you just prefer historic towns, rural traditions and a good helping of peace and tranquillity.

Three main areas to consider initially are:

1. The Black Sea coast

2. The ski resorts and mountain regions of the Rila, Rodophi or Pirin Mountains

3. The more rural areas of Bulgaria, one of the most popular being around the city of Veliko Tarnovo.

Unless you know exactly where you want to buy, researching the country, towns and villages is essential before committing to a purchase. There is so much property available, in so many areas, you can feel totally overwhelmed and it is easy to lose sight of your objectives so – before doing anything else – buy a map. Obvious, but often people look up maps on the internet and spend hours zooming in and out of little squares and don't ever get a real sense of the place. There's nothing more satisfying than spreading out a huge map on the floor or table to get a true feel of the country.

A great website for getting an initial feel for the geographical layout of Bulgaria is *www.bgmaps.com*. They've even included a little British flag so us Brits can understand it!

You can get maps of Bulgaria in most good good bookstores including *www.amazon.co.uk*

Many estate agents have websites that include a search facility for properties in specific areas and even in specific villages. On some sites it is possible to click on the property and it will show you exactly where it is situated in Bulgaria and other agents include a link to a specialist Bulgarian map site where if the name of the village is inserted into the search a detailed map will appear.

Another essential item is a travel guide, which will give you more detailed information about the towns and villages. *The Lonely Planet Guide*, *The Blue Guide to Bulgaria* and *The Rough Guide to Bulgaria* are the main three available at the moment.

BLACK SEA COAST

Bulgaria's coastline is on the Black Sea and developing fast. A large number of new construction projects have begun, and the coastline is in the process of dramatic change. Prices in some areas have risen nearly 25% in the last twelve months. The prices are expected to continue to rise in the foreseeable future, as more and more foreigners invest on the coast and the awareness of the desirability of the country grows and grows.

There are two main airports on the coast – one at Varna, which serves the northern coastline and one at Bourgas, which serves the south. Property prices are increasing rapidly in both these areas. Villas along the coastline north of Varna are very popular, however, an alternative option is to buy an apartment in the centre of Varna itself. The city has many local amenities and its own beaches. The Old Greek Quarter in the centre is very popular. Apartments bought here have the potential of being able to rent out all year round.

A new 50 square metre studio overlooking Kavarna Bay on the northern coastline, can be bought for approximately £22,500. A one bedroom apartment in a private complex with restaurants, bars, shops, swimming pools and health facilities can be bought in Sunny Beach on the Southern part of the Black Sea coast for approximately £31,500. Prices vary considerably and so do the different areas – some areas are modern and are constantly being developed – others are more historical and less developed. Make sure you choose an area that meets your requirements.

SKI RESORTS

A similar pattern of price rises is happening in the major ski resorts of Bansko, Borovets, Pamporovo and Mount Vitosha, near to the capital Sofia. The cost of skiing is comparatively low compared to the rest of Europe and new hotels and apartments are springing up in and around the main resorts in order to cater for the growing number of tourists.

Bansko

Bansko is the newest ski resort, and the most rapidly developing one. The town of Bansko is an ancient small town, with cobbled streets and many cultural monuments, surrounded by the majesty of the Pirin Mountains. About two and a half hours from Sofia airport, Bansko is fast becoming an all year round resort, with skiing and snowboarding in the winter and in the summer, visitors seek superb hiking, horseriding, and other outdoor sports combined with the fresh mountain air.

A brand new three–bedroom chalet can be bought for £40,000 to £45,000… A spacious and luxurious two–bed apartment including facilities such as a swimming pool, gym, sauna and restaurants could be found for £80,000, while a more basic one bedroom apartment in a smaller complex can be bought for around £35,000.

Borovets

Borovets is the oldest and the largest mountain resort in Bulgaria. It is located 1350m above sea level on the northern slopes of the Rila Mountains with vast pine forests. Borovets is at the foot of peak Mousala (2925m) the highest on the Balkan peninsula. It is easily accessible (just 75km from Sofia) and it takes about one and half hours to transfer from the airport.

There is major development planned for the future in and around Borovets. It is well worth checking before buying property in this area, just what is planned for the future. A recent article in the Sofia Echo newspaper reported that three major purpose built towns were going to be built to cater for the increasing number of tourists. Huge investment is pouring into the area around Borovets, including many local villages, so there are going to be some major changes to the landscape during the next few years.

Pamporovo

Located in the heart of the Rhodope mountains, Pamporovo is about 85km (one hour) from Plovdiv airport. Foreign investment is ploughing into the area and new ski runs are planned for the future linking local villages, with Pamporovo. Properties in this area can range from a rustic stone house in need of modernisation for just £10,000 right up to a brand new luxury three–bedroom chalet near to the resort for £55,000.

Vitosha Mountain (Sofia)

The Vitosha National Park incorporates Mount Vitosha, just 22km from the centre of Bulgaria's capital, Sofia. The park attracts numerous visitors both in summer and winter and is extremely popular for skiing at weekends, being so close to the capital. Property can be found to the south of Sofia, heading past Iskar Lake and on to the Rila Mountains. Lakeside properties can be found but they are few and far between. Again, prices range enormously and it is best to gain a knowledge of what you get for your money by trawling through the estate agents' details.

RURAL AREAS

In the more rural areas, property prices are much cheaper and although prices are on the increase, the rise is far less dramatic. Rural properties costing around £5,000 can be found across the whole of Bulgaria but, two of the main areas that are becoming more popular are the old medieval capital of Veliko Tarnovo, properties along the Danube River and homes around the major town of Ruse. If you are searching for beautiful countryside you are sure to find it in Central Bulgaria and the surrounding villages of the Stara Planina Mountain range which stretches almost the entire width of the country.

Veliko Tarnovo is the old medieval capital and has many cultural and heritage attractions. It's an attractive city perched on the hillside, with cobbled streets and traditional buildings, overlooking the Tsaravets Fortress on the hillside opposite. The surrounding villages still have a strong sense of community and many people still live off the land raising their own livestock. The locals are very friendly and are receptive to foreigners (including us Brits) coming to live amongst them. The city itself has plenty of restaurants and cafés and is home to one of the best Universities in Bulgaria. Property prices in this region are exceptionally low.

Buying a rural property, as in many other countries, is considerably cheaper than buying off plan. For the price tag of just £3,000, peace, tranquillity and rustic solitude are easily obtainable. For this price, the house would need to be renovated to bring it up to western standards, but with incredibly low building costs in Bulgaria, this makes "the rural choice" a more affordable option.

Traditional rustic houses often come with one or two large barns, on between 1000 and 3000 square metres of land. Many properties can be located within 20 minutes of the nearest town and also have water and electricity. The toilet, if there is one, will be a wooden hut at the end of the garden. The rural houses also have external stairs and because of the hot climate, summer kitchens are attached or near to the main property, with old clay ovens. Obviously if you want something totally away from civilisation – Bulgaria has that too – but be sure to check out the access as in winter many rural roads are unpassable. A habitable rural property that needs minor work can be acquired for between £12,000 to £15,000.

How To Buy A Property In Bulgaria

"An Increasing Number Of Britons Are
Investing In Property In Bulgaria."
– LIVERPOOL DAILY ECHO, FEB 2004

Restrictions On Brits & Other Foreigners

Currently, there are still restrictions on foreigners buying land in Bulgaria, but these restrictions are due to change soon as Bulgaria works towards complying with EU directives for joining the European Union in 2007.

At present, Bulgarian law dictates that foreign individuals are not allowed to own land in Bulgaria. If buying an apartment, this can be done as an individual as you will not actually own any land. However, if a house or villa with land is to be bought, then a limited company has to be set up.

On your first visit to Bulgaria, if you are going to be buying a house, then the first two things you must do are to open a Bulgarian bank account and set up a limited company.

OPENING A BANK ACCOUNT

Setting up an account is very simple and costs nothing. If there is an official at the bank who speaks English, then the process is fairly uncomplicated, but it can take time. However, if nobody speaks English, you don't stand a chance! Estate agents will offer to guide you through the process and will accompany you to the bank. If a joint account is required, then both parties have to be present at the time to sign all the relevant documentation.

Monthly banking charges in Bulgaria are approximately 80 pence per month. Internet banking is available in some, but not all, Bulgarian banks. This also has to be set up when you are in Bulgaria and there still seems to be a lot of teething troubles where people have been given their passwords but have not been able to access their accounts on return to the UK. A bank manager that can speak English is definitely a bonus.

It is wise to set up a sterling account so that sterling can be transferred from the UK, and also to set up an account in Leva, the Bulgarian currency. Money can then be transferred from the Bulgarian sterling account to the Leva account, which can be used to purchase items in Bulgaria and pay for utility bills at a future date. Money can be transferred directly from a UK bank account to a Bulgarian bank account easily upon return.

SETTING UP A LIMITED COMPANY

Setting up a company is a relatively easy process and can be organised in a day. Most estate agents organise this as part of the complete service they offer and it costs between £400 and £600. The bank certificate, showing that the minimum amount that has been deposited, is presented to the Court for registration to be processed, along with other company documents that are drawn up. Once the company has been registered, the company buys the property and owns the land and you are the sole owner of the company and respectively of the land.

The minimum starting capital that is required by Bulgarian law to establish a limited company is 5000 Leva (approximately £1,700 assuming an exchange rate of 2.88 Leva to the pound sterling) This is not the cost of setting up the company, just the amount required to be deposited in a bank account to show that you have a certain amount as a condition of setting up the company. This amount needs to be taken out on your trip so that you can deposit this and it can be used immediately for any deposit that is required or other costs.

The company does not have to operate or trade it is just a legal vessel to enable you to buy a property. Each year it will be necessary to declare the company accounts and this can be organised by an independant lawyer or the lawyer employed by your estate agent and costs approximately £50 to £70.

Estate agents will accompany you to the local Notary office where the Notary has to witness your signature on the company documents. The notary will charge for this and the fee is approximately £10. Two copies of the company documents are produced. One in the Bulgarian language and one in English. The lawyer should guide you through the contract word by word to explain the detail. The new company will also be registered with the National Tax Register Authority, National Companies Register and the National Social Security Institute.

An annual tax return for the company is required and this is due to be submitted by the end of March. Even if there has been no trading or profit, as will be the case if it is used solely for personal use, the company accounts still need to be declared. Any non–compliance or late return will incur an automatic fine, so ensure that your accountant submits the return in good time. If it is a very simple return, an accountant will charge between £30 to £50 for this, but again, prices vary enormously so the best advice is to shop around and obtain more than one quote.

CALCULATING YOUR BUDGET

"Mediterranean climate, average summer temperature 27° C
The fastest growing tourist destination market in Europe –
over 4 million visitors in 2003, up 21%"
– BULGARIAN TREASURY 2004

WHAT DO YOU NEED TO INCLUDE?

When budgeting for buying a property, estate agents fees also have to be allowed for, as both the buyer and the seller pay the estate agent in Bulgaria.

Estate agents fees are normally between 3% and 5% of the property purchase price, but some agents have been known to quote more. Many estate agents will quote a percentage fee but also quote a 'minimum' or 'not less than' price. This is because as a percentage fee, the agent would be making a relatively small amount of money on a property costing £3,000, for roughly the same work as a property costing £30,000. A 'minimum' or 'not less than' price can vary from agent to agent but is usually in the region of £350 to £500.

Estate agents offer a complete package for viewing and most will arrange flights, accommodation, and transfers. Some agents charge a daily viewing fee of between £30 and £100 which is fully refundable if a property is purchased from them, but more and more are now dropping this daily charge as competition increases. Nevertheless, many still charge a fee for the number of kilometres travelled during the viewing and this is usually about 20 eurocents (approximately 12 pence) per kilometre. But remember, if several rural properties are being viewed this can soon add up so this cost needs to be budgeted for.

Most estate agents offer to arrange the conveyancing for you or if you prefer, an independent lawyer can be employed. The overall fee will include their time spent communicating with the owner, research and surveys on the property, preparation of preliminary contracts and creating a further final contract for the completion of the sale. The costs for this can range upwards from £1000 if organised through an agent. Lists of lawyers can be found on the Bulgarian Embassy website... *www.bulgarianembassy.org.uk*

If you are buying an apartment 'off plan' then the estate agents' fees are usually due at the time you sign preliminary contracts rather than on completion, so you need to ensure that you have funds available at this time.

A municipal tax, which is the UK equivalent of stamp duty, is also payable. The municipal tax is currently 2% of the purchase price.

When buying an apartment, remember to take into account the additional cost of an annual maintenance and management fee. This covers the insurance of the building, maintenance of public areas such as communal gardens and swimming pool if there is one, caretaking and security. These are normally based on the size of the apartment. Currently, annual costs for maintenance can be anything from £5 to £10 per square metre.

When buying a house, in addition to these property related costs, don't forget to include in your budget the cost for setting up a limited company. This is between £400 and £600.

It is important to compare the total cost of buying a property with an agent, rather than simply comparing their percentage fees. Some agents charge for viewing, some do not; some refund if you purchase with them and others charge you a fee depending on how many kilometres you have travelled to view the properties.

That said, all these costs are extremely low in comparison to the UK.

Ensure that you check the prices of houses between the different estate agency websites. You sometimes find that the same house can be offered by a different agency at a higher price. Some more unscrupulous agents will artificially inflate prices. So, check out the reasons if the difference in the price of a house is more than 10%.

BUDGET CALCULATOR
(Print This Out & Fill It In)

Property Price ....

Municipal Tax (at 2%) ....

Estate Agent's Fee (at ...%) ....

Agent's Viewing fee ....

Travel (Flights/Car) ....

Conveyancing/Notary Fee ....

Setting Up Limited Company ....

Maintenance Charges ....

TOTAL COST ....

FINDING AN AGENT

"Average 2003 increase 23–28%, some areas increased 100% in 2003"
– SOFIA MORNING NEWS, FEB 2004

TOP TIPS FOR CHOOSING AN AGENT

Expect the levels of service to vary enormously from agent to agent. There has been a sudden and overwhelming interest in Bulgaria, and because of this, many estate agents are receiving hundreds and hundreds of enquiries a day. Some, but not all agents, are struggling to deal with this sudden growth and this can sometimes result in an apparent lack of organisational skills, a higher than average number of human errors and poor communication. There are however, other agents, that give an excellent level of service.

The Bulgarian Embassy in London has lists of estate agents operating in both the UK and Bulgaria and details of these can be accessed on–line. The Internet is a good place to start a general search, and one or two agents are now beginning to hold seminars in London.

Many properties on websites are snapped up extremely quickly. It is not unusual for an entire apartment block to be sold out in less than two weeks of being released. Some developers have responded to this huge demand by increasing the costs of the apartments after the first week, so you may find something you like one day and the day after, it may have risen by a few thousand pounds.

It's not just new builds that are selling quickly though; rural properties are also selling fast. Some people are actually "buying blind" from Internet sites – without even visiting Bulgaria to view the property. Buying blind is an enormously risky strategy and not to be recommended. The photos of the property may look fantastic, but when you see it in the flesh, you may be in for a shock. Rural properties, although incredibly good value, need a lot of renovation work in order to bring them up to Western standards.

THINKING OF BUYING BLIND?

Properties on many websites get snapped up extremely quickly. This leads some people to buy blind. Buying blind from internet sites is really not a good idea Despite beautiful photographs many rural properties will need a lot of renovation work and your bargain could soon turn into a liability.

Often properties that appear available on the internet, will be sold to someone else before you can even arrange your viewing trip. To avoid the disappointment of the 'home you have set your heart on' being sold before you can get on the plane, it is best to just 'get out there' to see what is available and arrange a viewing trip with one or more agents.

Viewing on the Internet is important research as it does help to gain a good knowledge of what types of property are available. It also gives an opportunity to compare prices in different areas. However, do not be fooled by attractive looking web sites that offer many properties. The best way to get an initial feel for a company and its abilities is to start communicating with them by phone or email. You should get a feel for their level of professionalism from their responses.

More and more rural properties are becoming available on a daily basis so there is a large choice and there is no need to rush into buying something and regretting it later – just because it appears to be the ideal property and the bargain of the century. There are numerous good value houses on the market and more coming on to the market each day.

When choosing an agent, ensure that they provide effective after–sales service. Buying a property overseas is only the start of the process and you may need to ensure that the agent is able to offer services such as; payment of bills in your absence, preparation of annual company accounts, assistance in obtaining resident permits, property management and very importantly, if you are buying a house that needs renovation, the ability to provide support if you are looking for a builder.

AGENTS I'VE USED...

I've included details of a few agents I've
used below for your reference but please use your
own judgement when choosing an agent.

Nick Parkin (*www.bg–aa.com*)
Stephane Lambert (*www.stara–planina.com*)
Sebastian Kinsman (*www.balkanskichalets.com*)

VIEWING

"Sofia Residential Property Market Sees Rising Demand"
– SOFIA MORNING NEWS, FEB 2004

One village can differ considerably from the next so viewing the surroundings is just as important as viewing the property. There is a Government initiative called 'Beautiful Bulgaria' in which towns and villages are encouraged to spruce up their surroundings. Some villages have benefited enormously and are indeed cleaner, tidier, and more welcoming for tourists and foreign visitors. Others still look like ghost towns. Viewing the village is as important as viewing the property.

Access to the property must also be considered, as in summer months the roads, although incredibly potholed, are at least clear. In the winter months it is a totally different story and many rural roads are totally impassable due to the heavy snowfalls. Being totally cut off from civilisation for a few months is a real possibility.

It is very easy to get 'punch drunk' when viewing many properties in one day. At the beginning of a trip, it may be easy to remember the details of each property that is viewed. At the end of the trip, totally exhausted, it may be difficult to remember which property was your favourite. Writing a few notes on each of the property details, describing any feelings about the property, and likes and dislikes, may be a good reminder later on. Taking digital photographs and even video means that if you get confused and totally overwhelmed, you can look through your notes as a reminder when feeling more refreshed.

Estate agents offer a complete package for viewing and most will arrange flights, accommodation, and transfers. Some agents charge a daily viewing fee of between £30 and £100 which is fully refundable if a property is purchased from them.

VIEWING CHECKLIST
(Print This Out For Each Property You View & Don't Forget To Take Photos)

Property

- ❑ Price _____
- ❑ Bedrooms _____
- ❑ Area (internal) _____
- ❑ Area (land) _____
- ❑ Gas?
- ❑ Electricity?
- ❑ Water?

Notes (maintenance tasks, pros/cons etc):

Location

- ❑ Rural
- ❑ Coast
- ❑ Mountain
- ❑ Ski Resort

Notes (noise level, state of surrounding villages etc):

Access

- ❑ Poor
- ❑ Fair
- ❑ Good

Additional Notes

THE LEGAL PROCESS

"Some developers have seen their tourist property complexes rise in value in excess of a colossal 100% in a year! Even if spread across the board, it still averages out to a sizeable capital growth of 35%"
WWW.NOVINITE.COM, NOV 2004

GENERAL BUYING INFORMATION

A list of Bulgarian lawyers can be obtained from the British Embassy if you choose to employ an independent lawyer. One way to gain a personal recommendation, is to join one of the website forums and post a notice of your request. Like any other country, Bulgaria has some lawyers that are better than others, so a good personal recommendation is worth its weight in gold if one can be obtained.

Generally speaking, negotiation on house prices is not widespread. However, there is no reason why a lower price should not be suggested, even if it is not accepted. A check to see what other similar properties in the area have been sold for is always a good guide.

When a property has been found and the purchase price agreed, the lawyer will then draw up a preliminary contract setting out all the agreed

26

details and setting out the initial amount of deposit to be paid. This is usually about 10%, whether a brand new apartment or villa is being bought or an older property. When the deposit has been paid, this usually ensures that the property is taken off the market, however, it should be made conditional, upon signing the preliminary contract, to cover against any unscrupulous vendors.

SURVEYS AND SEARCHES

A lawyer or agent will contact the owners to arrange a survey and also complete the research on the property, including checking court records and mortgage records. Normally a visual survey will be arranged and the cost of this is often included in your overall fee to your lawyer or estate agent. A structural engineer will view the property to inspect the construction. A full structural survey can be arranged if it is a particularly old house or there is some doubt about the land that the building has been built on. This type of survey usually involves a geologist taking soil samples to inspect the condition of the land and foundations.

PRELIMINARY AND FINAL CONTRACTS

When buying an 'off plan' property, a preliminary contract will include conditions such as deadlines for completion of the shell, roof, and final date for finishing all construction work. Details of the construction materials used are set out, together with payment options agreed to. Payments are made in instalments, as the various stages of construction of the new building are finished. A delivery acceptance record will have to be signed upon completion, to say that you are happy with the standard of construction and finishing. Any defects or problems must be pointed out at this stage to enable the construction agency to rectify these.

Preliminary contracts are drawn up within a couple of weeks of agreeing to purchase.

For 'off plan' property, your first stage payment will be due when you sign the preliminary contract. Do remember that you are liable to lose the property, and your deposit, if you are late in making your payments. Preliminary contracts will be sent to you in the UK for signing.

The developer will give you a completion date and it is usually written into the preliminary contract that the developer will be eligible to pay penalties if this deadline is not adhered to.

If you are visiting Bulgaria and have found a suitable house, you do not have to remain in Bulgaria to sign the preliminary contracts but can give power of attorney to the lawyer to sign these on your behalf. The final contract is then drawn up and both buyer and seller meet at the public notary office and the final contract signing is witnessed. Again, you do not have to be present if power of attorney is given to the lawyer. The whole process can usually be done within a month if required.

When a date for the final completion is agreed upon, it is possible to bring the date forward, but it is not possible to move it back, so it is imperative that finances are (or will be) in place to complete by the agreed date. Any time scales agreed upon must be realistic, as failure to complete as agreed, will incur large penalties, and possible loss of the purchase of the property.

After the deposit on a house has been paid, the remaining balance of the purchase price needed for completion can be transferred to a Bulgarian Bank account from the UK.

The Title Deeds should be expected to be received a week or two after the final completion date. The originals will be written in Bulgarian but an English translation can be requested for a small extra cost.

There may be some discrepancy on the actual price paid for the property, and the price on the Title Deeds. In Bulgaria there is a "tax estimation price" and a "purchase price". The tax estimation price is much lower than the actual "purchase price". This is for the purpose of taxation. Most Bulgarian property owners will want the lower "taxation price" written in the title deed, rather than the "actual price" which is being paid for the property. This is in fact illegal but still common practice, as in some other European countries, but most estate agents will discourage this practice.

If the property is occupied, do not expect the owners to have moved out for the completion date as in the UK. In Bulgaria, the usual term for the incumbent owners of the property to move out after completion of the sale is one month. This could be negotiated if the buyers require a shorter term. If this is the case, ask the estate agents to assist with any negotiations – but do not expect to move in on the day of final completion.

YOUR FIRST VISIT

"Tourist Flow to Bulgaria Grows by 16.28%"

– WWW.NOVINITE.COM, NOV 2004

COMMUNICATION

One of the most important things to remember is that the Bulgarians shake their heads from side to side when they mean 'yes' and nod when they mean 'no'.

It is advisable to listen carefully to the spoken words 'da' which means yes, and 'ne' which means no. If Bulgarians know they are speaking to Brits, sometimes the nodding and shaking can be reversed which further adds to the confusion and general misunderstanding.

You will find English speaking Bulgarians in most major cities and larger towns but on the whole, Bulgarian is the national language and is spoken everywhere. A really useful item to take with you is a guide that has a translation for the Bulgarian alphabet. The Cyrillic alphabet is used which bears hardly any resemblance to our Latin alphabet.

In the ski areas and on the coast you will almost certainly find some people that speak English, however, English is not widely spoken in the more rural areas.

DON'T GET MIXED UP

Bulgarians shake their head for "yes" and nod for "no". To confuse matters further some Bulgarians, in an effort to be helpful, will swap this custom around when they're talking to Brits!

You will find English speaking estate agents and lawyers and other professional people but if you buy a property and then want to employ a gardener, local builder or any sort of daily help, a little knowledge of Bulgarian is a necessity. On most occasions, you will almost certainly find someone who speaks English that can translate for you.

English is the most common second language, especially among the young, followed by German and French, but these are not widely spoken.

FLIGHTS

Direct international flights are available to the capital, Sofia, all year round. Direct charter flights to the Black Sea airports of Varna and Burgas are available from late April until early October only. Flights take just a little over three hours and you can fly from many UK airports. It is important to remember that flights to coastal airports are usually for either 7 or 14 days, so a quick viewing trip over the weekend is not a possibility at the moment, unless you fly to Sofia and take an internal flight. Often it is cheaper to find a 'package' deal with a tour operator than to book flights and accommodation separately.

The cost of flights to Sofia are approximately £200 to £250, however, a flight to the coast at the beginning or end of the summer season can be found for just £75 return.

If you are visiting the coast off–season there are numerous internal flights from Sofia to Varna and Burgas. If Veliko Tarnovo is your destination, a bus journey from Sofia will take about three to four hours but it is probably much easier for the estate agent to arrange a taxi for you.

Visas

You can visit Bulgaria for up to 30 days without a visa within a six–month period. However, for longer stays you will have to apply for either a short–term or long–term visa. These can be obtained from The Embassy of the Republic of Bulgaria, 186–188 Queen's Gate, London SW7 5HL or visit their website *www.bulgarianembassy.org.uk*, where visa application forms can be downloaded.

A type C (short–term visa) enables you to stay up to 90 days within each period of six months. If you require a longer period or want to apply for a residence permit then a type D (long–term) visa must be applied for.

A type D, long–term visa is only valid for single entry and is for a stay of up to 90 days. It is valid for up to six months from the date of issue. It is issued for those who intend to apply for a long–term or permanent residence permit for Bulgaria.

Driving in Bulgaria

Hiring a car is another option and a good network of roads gives access to major cities and towns. However, roads in the more rural areas are not well made and – beware the famous Bulgarian pothole! There are lots of them. Finding your way around can often be impossible as you move away from the coast or major ski resorts as most of the road signs are cleverly written in Cyrillic so you probably won't know where you are going or how far it is! You will need a map that has the name of the villages in Cyrillic as well as English. Some of the major road signs on the coast and in and around Sofia are in English.

Bulgarians drive on the right hand side (most of the time). Avoiding potholes is the major distraction and this is when you will find cars approaching you on the same side that you are driving on. Other hazards include livestock and horse–drawn carts on the roads, especially during the spring and summer months. Conditions deteriorate during the winter and night driving is not usually advised – many motorists often drive with very dim or even no headlights at all.

You will need a current European driving licence and of course, full, comprehensive insurance is recommended.

GETTING AROUND

Buses link all major towns and villages. The local buses, run by the Government, are frequent and inexpensive. Private bus companies run the longer distance routes. These buses are newer and more comfortable than the local government buses but are still incredibly reasonably priced. A three–hour journey from the coast, inland to Veliko Tarnovo, for instance, would cost just £4. Taxis are available in all major towns and are run on meters. Local journeys around town work out at about 30p.

The network of railways does extend to most major cities but standards are not as high as you would expect in western and northern Europe. However, trains are usually comfortable, reasonably quick and astoundingly cheap. There is an excellent inter–city express service between Sofia, Varna and Bourgas.

CURRENCY AND RESTRICTIONS

The unit of currency in Bulgaria is the Lev, the plural is Leva. The Lev is divided into one hundred Stotinki. Leva is invariably shortened to lv on price tags. Prices for smaller items are not written as 40 Stotinki but 0.4lv. When paying for something in a shop, do not always expect to receive the right change – often the price is rounded up to the nearest Lev. In official and business documents you may see the currency written as BGN instead of Leva.

Credit cards are not widely accepted yet in Bulgaria except in the much larger hotels and restaurants that cater to foreign tourists. Cash machines are widespread and do take major credit and debit cards.

The Leva is linked to the Euro and house prices are often quoted in Euros.

There are restrictions on taking currency into Bulgaria. The maximum that is allowed is up to 5000 Leva (approximately £1,750.00) without submitting a customs declaration and up to 25,000 Leva (approximately £8,750.00) by submitting a customs declaration and a detailed bank statement proving the origin of funds.

CURRENCY COMPARISON...

GBP		BGN
£ 1.00	=	Lv 2.80

Rates vary and are subject to change. Visit *www.xe.com/ucc* for most up–to–date exchange rates

EATING OUT

Eating out is a complete pleasure as the restaurant bill will be lower than you have ever experienced in the UK. A huge mixed salad, a glass of wine and a bottle of mineral water for lunch can be just £1.20. A three-course meal in the evening with wine would be just £5.00.

A bottle of wine can be bought from 80 pence in a restaurant, although a better quality one might cost £1.50 to £2.00. A bottle of beer would be just 30 pence. A 'morning coffee break' in a cafe, could cost as little as 12 pence for an espresso.

The best thing about Bulgarian cuisine is the abundance of fresh fruit and vegetables. The food is delicious and varied. There are many traditional Bulgarian dishes that have a Greek or Turkish influence.

 For breakfast, especially in the mountain areas, you can taste pancakes with fresh fruit berries and a delicious syrup. One of the most popular Bulgarian breakfasts is 'Banitsa', a hot, baked cheese pastry. Bulgaria is also famous for its yoghurt and honey.

For lunch the Bulgarians love their salads and most restaurants offer more than a dozen to choose from. A 'Shopska' salad is typical of the more traditional, which includes chopped tomatoes, cucumbers, onions, feta cheese and olives.

For dinner, Kavarna is a traditional dish of meat and vegetables roasted in an earthenware dish with lots of garlic, onions, tomatoes, oil and spices. Popular dishes include kebahche (grilled spicy meat sausages) and kyufte – sausages that are flattened but curled round in a circle.

FACTS AND FIGURES ABOUT BULGARIA

"Bulgaria already has a well–developed network of national parks and protected areas and supports some of the richest biodiversity in Europe."

– THE GUARDIAN, SEP 2004

FOREIGN INVESTMENT, WORK PERMITS & RESIDENCY

Bulgaria is roughly the same size as England and is located on the Balkan Peninsula surrounded by the Black Sea to the east, Romania to the north, Serbia and Macedonia to the West and Greece and Turkey to the South. Living in Bulgaria provides numerous opportunities for easy excursions into the surrounding countries and of course, there is the tremendous beauty of Bulgaria itself to explore, and a much slower pace of life to savour.

The varied landscape features 240 miles of coastline, the Rila and Rhodope mountain ranges and the Stara Planina mountain range which stretches from Sofia across Bulgaria to the coast. The Danube River is the border to the north and there are many lakes, rivers and national parks throughout the country.

Bulgaria has a population of 8.4 million and is divided into 28 districts and 250 municipalities. The capital, Sofia has 1.2 million inhabitants.

Nearly 87% of the country's inhabitants follow the Bulgarian Orthodox religion. The remainder are Muslims, and there are small numbers of Catholics and other Christian sects. Bulgaria has many monasteries, the most famous of which is at Rila.

The main airport is situated in Sofia with further airports at Plovdiv and on the coast at Varna and Bourgas. Bulgaria is two hours ahead of GMT and a flight there takes just over three hours.

Bulgaria experiences cold, usually snowy winters, and long hot, dry summers where temperatures can reach over 30 degrees centigrade. Autumn and spring are also generally quite mild.

GOVERNMENT AND FOREIGN INVESTMENT

A former communist country, Bulgaria is now governed under a parliamentary democracy. In 1996 Bulgaria experienced the fall of the socialist government as a result of a major economic downturn. But, since a democracy has been in place, Bulgaria has been committed to economic reform and has experienced steady economic growth.

The head of state is the President of the Republic, assisted by a Vice President, both of whom are elected every five years. There are parliamentary elections every four years, and the present head of parliament is Prime Minister Saxe–Coburg. He actually became King of Bulgaria when he was six and was then exiled at the age of nine, returning to Bulgaria some 55 years later to be elected by his people as Prime Minister.

Bulgaria joined NATO in 2004 and is striving towards proposed accession to the European Union in 2007.

Foreign investment has poured into Bulgaria in 2003 and 2004. An increase of 43.7% was experienced in the first three months of 2003 compared to the same period in 2002. The rates of taxation are very low compared to the rest of Europe.

Annual inflation is currently at 3.8% and the country enjoys one of the highest economic growth rates in Europe at 4.5%.

WORK PERMITS, RESIDENCY AND INCOME TAX

Two types of residence permit can be granted: A temporary permit, for residency of up to a year, or a permanent one.

To obtain a temporary residence permit you need a Type D visa and also proof of National Insurance or social security. You also require a minimum of 3000 Leva (approximately £1020) deposited in a Bulgarian bank account. It is granted for one year and is renewed each year, together with a Bulgarian Identity Card.

To obtain a permanent residence one must spend at least 5 years in Bulgaria under the long–term stay conditions with a temporary residence permit.

To ascertain whether or not you would be eligible for a permit it is best to consult the Bulgarian Embassy in London who will give details of the conditions under which you can apply.

If you intend to work in Bulgaria then there is a progressive rate of income tax of between 15% and 29%. If you are a "permanent resident" of Bulgaria, tax will be calculated both on your income earned in Bulgaria and overseas. If you are not a permanent resident and are only working in Bulgaria temporarily, then tax is only payable on your income earned whilst there. In 2004 the rate of standard Corporation tax is 19.5%.

OTHER COSTS OF LIVING IN BULGARIA

LOCAL TAXES

Once you own a property, local annual taxes have to be paid. These are incredibly low in comparison to the UK. The annual rate of tax on a house is 0.15% of the purchase price. So if a house has been purchased for £10,000 the annual tax payable would be £15.

The only other tax to pay is a garbage tax and this varies depending on the location and size of the house, but is in the region of £10 to £20 per year.

If an apartment is bought, local taxes are still due, together with annual maintenance and management fees that have been set by the developer or managing agent.

UTILITIES

Apart from in the capital, Sofia, the gas system network is not developed in Bulgaria. The main form of heating is electricity and in the rural areas, wood burning stoves are a much cheaper way to heat a house. A telephone service is widely available across Bulgaria.

Both water and electricity supplies can be organised via the Municipal offices. An official comes round each month to check water and electric and the bills can be paid through the local post office. There is no standing charge for utilities apart from telephones. Water and electricity bills can also be paid direct to the company via a direct debit set up at the local branch of the bank, but this has to be arranged via the Municipal office.

PROPERTY INSURANCE

You will need to organise house and contents insurance. Your estate agent may offer this service. But as the cost of living in Bulgaria is extremely low, it's cheap compared to the prices you would pay in the UK. For instance, house and contents insurance would be between £70 and £150 per year, depending of course on the type of house and value of goods listed on the contents.

For a property costing in the region of £20,000, insurance against theft, flood and fire costs about £100 annually with a good, reliable insurance company. Cheaper insurance, of course, can always be obtained and costs do vary from company to company, but this is a good general guide.

DRIVING COSTS

Driving a car in Bulgaria is inexpensive too. The cost of a litre of petrol is just 50 pence and LPG just 25 pence per litre. Most of the cars in Bulgaria are equipped with LPG systems so cars are mostly fuelled with the non–pollutant and very cheap propane gas. Diesel fuel is also widely available throughout the country.

Cars are amongst the cheapest in Europe to buy. A brand new four–wheel drive costs £6,000 and a brand new Renault Clio just £4,000.

Your existing European driving licence is all that is required to drive a car in Bulgaria. There are a few annual fees to be paid which include driver responsibility insurance; which is about £12 per year, road tax, depending on the engine power is about £32 per year and an MOT costs just £8.

RENOVATION, RENTAL & RE–SALE

RENOVATION

If you intend renovating a property, building costs are comparatively low in Bulgaria compared with the rest of Europe. An average Bulgarian wage is currently £100 per month. Rates for employing builders differ widely but as a guide, building works cost approximately one third of what it would cost in the UK. Often estate agents can arrange building quotes for you, but it is always wise to obtain at least three quotes.

If the intention is to build a new property on the plot and demolish the old, then average prices for new building works are between £150 and £250 per square meter. The cost of building works seem to be following the trend in property prices – they are on the increase, as more and more people discover the tremendously good value of property and land in Bulgaria.

RENTAL AND RE–SALE

As the popularity of Bulgaria continues to grow, the rental market is following suit. The most frequently visited destination in Bulgaria is the Black Sea Coast but the mountain and rural areas are not far behind. With costs of skiing in Bulgaria being much lower than in the rest of Europe, there is an increase in demand for rental property in the ski resorts and surrounding villages. Holidays where you can get 'away from it all' to take time to explore nature and enjoy a much slower pace of life are also on the increase.

Rental income varies considerably from area to area. On the coast, months for letting are typically from May to September. The ski resorts have a winter rental season of about four months, and the traditional Bulgarian town of Bansko, the newest ski resort, has potential for rental returns all year round offering mountain biking and hiking during the summer months and traditional outdoor activities.

There is also the opportunity to buy apartments in Sofia, the capital, where rental incomes are increasing rapidly.

Letting agents are just beginning to become established in Bulgaria and some have contracts with the major tour operators who will handle all of the management and bookings for you for a fee. Fees are typically between 20% and 30% of gross rental income.

Some brand new apartments are now actually being sold with an annual guaranteed rental income, usually of about 8%.

CAPITAL GAINS TAX

If a property is bought for investment and profit only, there is a capital gains tax if a property is sold again before a five year term and this is currently 19.5%. Fees to the estate agent would also be incurred.

Sample Property Purchasing Costs

Traditional rustic house near to major town

Property Price	£6000.00
Stamp Duty (municipal tax) at 2%	£120.00
Estate Agent Fees at 5%	£300.00
Lawyer/Conveyancing/Notary Fee	£1000.00
Setting Up Company	£ 500.00
TOTAL COST	£7,920.00

Two bedroom 'off plan' apartment (106 square metres) in apartment complex on the coast with sea views

Property Price	£75,000.00
Stamp Duty (municipal tax) at 2%	£1,500.00
Estate Agent Fees at 5%	£3,750.00
Annual Maintenance	£470.00
TOTAL COST	£80,720.00

One bedroom 'off plan' apartment (65 square metres) in a ski resort

Property Price	£33,500.00
Stamp Duty (municipal tax) at 2%	£760.00
Estate Agent Fees at 5%	£1675.00
Annual Maintenance	£455.00
TOTAL COST	£36,390.00

87 TIPS FROM A BRIT THAT HAS...

1. The bigger picture

Before doing anything – buy a map – obvious – but a lot of people don't do it – and struggle looking at a computer screen trying to make sense of it all in little squares. There's nothing better than unfolding a huge map and getting a sense of the 'whole country' and how it relates to the rest of the universe.

Maps to buy: *GeoCenter Euro Map of Bulgaria* is a great map but says on the front that it includes city plans of Veliko Tarnovo – it does not! It contains city maps of Sofia, Plovdiv and the coastal resorts. I'd also suggest getting the *Bulgaria Cartographia*

2. What are you looking for?

If you are looking to find a certain village or town then there's a good search facility on *www.bgmaps.com*. Don't be put off when it appears in Bulgarian – click on the union jack and all will become clear. The site has detailed maps of all the major Bulgarian cities and will also show you the nearest 5 peaks, springs, churches, caves, ports and lakes – how cool is that? There is also a route search facility.

3. Get a guide book

There are several guides available but the most helpful I found was *The Lonely Planet Guide* available from most bookshops and the internet. It was useful for giving you a general feel of the place but also gave specific details about many of the larger villages. Other guides include: *The Blue Guide to Bulgaria*, *The Rough Guide to Bulgaria*.

5. Just one click away

There's absolutely masses of research on the web that you can do – but ask yourself at the beginning, just how much do I really need to know and be specific about your information gathering. You can spend days, weeks, months, doing more and more research – but the best research is to get on the plane and get out there.

6. Been there, done it – how can I help?

Forums are an excellent way of gaining knowledge and learning from the experience of other people who have been there and done it – a huge amount of first hand knowledge at the touch of a button. Particularly useful when you get down to the nitty gritty of wanting an electrician or plumber or someone to do your dry stone walling. But be clear that one man may praise an estate agent to the hilt – whilst another may knock him to the ground – depends on your experience and you only ever know half the story. So just beware that not all you read may be what you will end up experiencing. In my opinion, one of the best forums is: *www.britsinbulgaria.com*

7. Explore, explore, explore

Bulgaria is a country with vastly different landscapes and climate. It can take a while to decide which area is the right area for you. Bulgaria has it all: green rolling hills, rocky mountains, marvellous beaches , flat plains as far as the eye can see. What do you want to be looking at? Make sure you are clear about which area you want to be in and check out the details. For a good overview of the country go to : *www.bulgariatravel.org*

8. Quiet night in

The cost of living is low – so budgeting for meals out should be a joy not a headache. With beer at 15p a bottle, wine at 80p a bottle and a coffee just 12p there's absolutely no excuse for a quiet night in. A delicious mixed salad – and I mean delicious, a half bottle of wine, with a bottle of mineral water cost me just £1.20. It was just so nice to be able to say – Yes, yes of course you can have another icecream kids – have as many as you want. I did of course, apply the same principal to the wine. £5 will cover the cost of an evening meal with wine – unless of course you want to have a complete blow out.

9. Facts and figures

If you like your facts and figures and want to know the finer details about Bulgaria then take a look at *www.fco.gov.uk*, the Foreign Commonwealth Office. If it's general property advice you are wanting then *www.bulgarian–property.org* offer a comprehensive guide to the whole property buying process – wherever you are buying. You can either download the e–book or send off for the CD.

10. If you feel the need

If you ever need to write a letter in Bulgarian – or just want to see how your name looks in cyrillic – then this link is a real goody – just type in what you want to say in the top box and it appears in the cyrillic alphabet in the box below. Simple. It's not a direct translation – it translates latin alphabet to cyrillic alphabet – but it's good enough to get a message across. *www.uni–bonn.de/967Emanfear/cyrlatencoder.php*

11. Read all about it.

News, business, life and leisure, sport – if you want to know whats going on in Bulgaria then you can read the Sofia Echo on line at *www.sofiaecho.com*.

12. When to go

Think about the time of year you wish to visit. If you are on a budget, fares to coastal airports are much cheaper at the beginning and end of the season in May and September/October. The weather can be beautiful and much cooler for viewing. At the moment, you can fly direct to the coastal airports in the summer season. Otherwise, you have to fly to Sofia and get a connecting internal flight. Bulgaria Air flies each day to Sofia (*www.balkanair.com*), as does British Airways (*www.ba.com*). Flights range from about £165 to £240.

13. Time to explore

If you are not clear about exactly where you want to buy then you will need as much time as possible to explore the country – two weeks minimum – more if you can – there's a huge range of landscapes, some like the Alps, some like the Dordogne, others like Tuscany, some areas as flat as a pancake as far as the eye can see. Unless you have your sights set on a particular area – you will need as much time as possible to explore.

14. Don't make assumptions.

Don't make an assumption you can just go over there for a few days. You can – but it is far easier and cheaper to get a flight for 7 or 14 days than for 3 or 4. The coastal airports especially are not up and running for 3 or 4 day visits and you can ONLY go for 7 or 14 to these airports. You can however, fly to Sofia, the capital for a few days but the cost is far greater.

15. To be direct

A direct flight to Bulgaria takes a little over 3 hours – you can go indirectly and sometimes this can be cheaper but boy can it be a longwinded operation. Some indirect flights can take up to seven hours. Others aren't too bad – Czech airlines appear to do a quick stop over and then onto Bulgaria. Don't forget that Bulgarian is 2 hours ahead of GMT.

16. Other airports may be nearer

Depending on where you wish to view – don't forget you can also fly to Istanbul and Bucharest airports – check out the map – they may be nearer to where you want to go than the Bulgarian Airports.

17. The scenic way

If you can't get a flight – or are on a tight budget – there is a coach service from Victoria London to Sofia. Balkan Horn and National Express go there – and it takes just over 50 hours. I believe Balkan Horn are the cheaper of the two. Just think of all that lovely scenery you would otherwise miss out on.

18. Nerves of steel

Driving – you will need nerves of steel, eyes peeled at all times and a sixth sense. Potholed roads, poor road markings and frankly, alarming driving practices coupled with erratic horse–drawn carts and numerous stray dogs make driving the ultimate challenge.

19. Be Brave

So if you have decided that you still wish to hire a car – then you can do so with all the well known companies such as Avis or Hertz and also some local Bulgarian ones which I found just as good and a lot cheaper. I used *www.rentacarbulgaria.com*

20. All fuelled up

Make sure you remember where the hire car people write down the number/letter of the fuel that your hired car uses. When you get to the petrol station – its not obvious which is the petrol, which is the diesel and which is the unleaded. Write down the number on a separate piece of paper and keep it handy to avoid lots of reversing and manoeuvring in the garage trying to decipher what's written on the pumps.

21. Finding your way

If you intend to drive in Bulgaria – finding your way around is extremely difficult as all the road signs and village signs are in cyrillic. Do not underestimate how difficult it is to navigate your way around the country. At several points you will not know where you are going, where you are, or even where you have been. There are two things that you will need. Make sure you have a map where the names of the villages are written in cyrillic – and also a bulgarian cyrillic alphabet/ latin alphabet comparison. I found the alphabet translation in the back of a guide book. You can then slam on the brakes as you approach the sign, pull over to the side, read the cyrillic letters on the sign one by one and write down the latin alphabet equivalent. A long–winded process but at least you know where you are in English and you can find the cyrillic name on the map – if you are lucky. Its useful to have someone with you for this purpose. Children will do – my children thought this was an excellent game.

22. Accommodation

Hotels are comparatively inexpensive to the rest of Europe – but if you want decent bathroom facilities then go for three or four stars rather than two. Rural accommodation is even cheaper and I stayed in a beautiful traditionally built hotel with my two children for just £20 per night.

For a cheap alternative to town hotels, a large selection of beautiful rural properties can be found at *www.ruralbulgaria.com*

23. Visas

You don't need a visa to visit Bulgaria. You can stay for up to 30 days without a visa. You can return again for another 30 days but you have to leave the country first. However, if you need to visit for longer you can apply to the embassy here for a 90 day tourist visa. You can apply on–line at *www.bulgarianembassy.org.uk*

24. 100 Stinkers

The unit of currency in Bulgaria is the Bulgarian lev – the plural is leva. There are 100 stotinki to the lev – my children called them 'stinkers' for short.

"Leva" is invariably shortened to lv on price tags. Prices for smaller items are not written as 40 stotinki but 0.4lv. In official and business documents, you may see the currency written as BGN instead of leva.

25. Prices

House prices may be quoted in euros and the leva is linked to the euro for the economy. But in the shops and restaurants you pay in leva. When paying for something in a shop – do not always expect to get the right change – often the price is rounded up to the nearest lev. BEWARE – if you do take euros for some reason and you have them in the same wallet or purse as leva – the 10 leva note looks extremely similar to the 10 euro note when you're not fully concentrating!

26. Adding it all up

Make sure you take a calculator with you. You may find yourself constantly trying to change from sterling to euros to leva, back to euros etc etc. House prices are quoted in euros and sometimes leva so it's far easier if you have a small calculator to hand.

27. Travellers cheques

If you take the money you need to set up your company and you take it in travellers cheques then make sure you take the biggest denomination possible. Some banks charge commission for each cheque changed and if you have £2000 in £20 denominations – you will be signing them forever. Sterling is easy enough to change in bureaus on the street in the larger towns or at the bank.

28. Shut your eyes when asking directions

DO remember – Bulgarians nod their heads when they say no and shake their heads when they say yes. It is especially confusing if you are asking directions. I met several 'terribly helpful' Bulgarians who realised the cultural difference and so compensated for this and changed their ways to ours – which is even MORE confusing – you just haven't got a clue. My tip – shut your eyes when you ask a question so that you only HEAR the answer. It's Da for yes and Ne for no.

29. Hotels/Accommodation

Accommodation is relatively cheap in Bulgaria compared to the rest of Europe. Some useful websites are: *www.sofiahotels.com www.sofiaapartments.com, www.varnahotels.com, www.varnaapartments.com, www. bourgashotels.com, www. plovdivhotels.com* and *www.beachbulgaria.com* for hotels and inclusive holidays

30. Hunt them out

Tourist information centres are supposed to be the easiest thing to find when you arrive at a new destination – not so in Bulgaria. Even if you have an address or some directions. I spent a week in Veliko Tarnovo and couldn't find the information centre. It wasn't me – honest – I found lots of others who couldn't find it too. Duh! More information about tourist information places can be found on the Official Tourism Site: *www.bulgariatravel.org*

31. Getting around

Estate agents can organise your transfer from the airport for you and if you see the tips on driving – this is a far better option if you don't want to explore the whole country but just need to get to your destination. Local taxis are on a meter and a local journey around town will be about 40p – but, as anywhere else in the world – you are a tourist – so many will try to charge you more, especially when arriving at the airport. Buses are an alternative and its hard to find the right bus if you don't speak the language – but if you find someone who speaks English that can help you – buses are a much cheaper alternative if you are travelling long distance. I travelled from the black sea coast of Bourgas to Veliko Tarnovo for just £4.

32. Carry a packet of tissues with you at all times

Hotels provide toilet paper but its rarely available anywhere else. Always carry tissues with you. Toilets in most restaurants are the european sit down variety but elsewhere its just the middle eastern "holes in the ground". The small bins near the toilets are for the paper – as throwing it down the toilet is a sure fire way of blocking it. The standard of toilets at bus and train stations are not even on the scale of 1 to 10. To use the toilet you will be charged 10 or 20 stotinskis and maybe another 10 or 20 for two sheets of toilet roll.

33. Looking for love, drinking with the locals or visiting a native?

For girls who are looking for boys, and boys who are looking for girls – make sure you check out the right hand. Married Bulgarians wear their wedding ring on their RIGHT hand not their left. If you are drinking a toast with Bulgarians "Naz drave" is "good health to you" BUT as you clink your glass you must look the person in the eye. It's considered rude if you don't. If there are six people at the table then you have to do this with each one. Do take flowers if you are visiting locals – however don't take even numbers – that is only appropriate for funerals – make sure the total is an odd number.

34. Remote buying – why not blindfold yourself and stick a pin on it?

A word first about remote buying – buying based on the photo on the agents website, putting a deposit on, without even having seen it. Ask yourself – would you ever do this in England? Next – can you afford to lose the deposit if it turns out not to be what you thought. You may as well blindfold yourself and stick a pin on the screen for all it's worth. I saw several properties I fell in love with when I saw the photo and description which I later viewed and was horrified when I saw the 'real thing'. Others that looked drab on the photo, were better by miles. Take the tip – that's why you bought this book – you REALLY need to see it for yourself.

35. Working out your budget – what can you afford?

Compare TOTAL costs for buying a property as property prices, company set up fees and agents commission vary enormously from agent to agent. Costs to consider: price of property, percentage commission for estate agent (usually between 3% and 5% and some have a minimum standard charge), legal costs (service often offered by estate agents), stamp duty 2%, mileage for viewing or daily viewing charge (often refundable)

Add to this of course cost of flights, transfers and accommodation and bear in mind that maybe you are going to need more than one trip! But think of it as an investment – not a cost.

36. Narrowing the search

There are SO many rural properties in Bulgaria – you could spend the rest of your life looking round, visiting numerous areas, all over the country. Unless you have six to ten weeks to do this you need to find ways of narrowing your search and defining exactly what you want. Use your guide–books and the travel websites to research different areas to see what appeals most to you.

37. Completely cut off

Consider EXACTLY how rural you want to be! Do you want to be miles from anyone (a lovely thought) or do you want to be at least 15 minutes away from a doctor, shop and cafe? How far do you want to travel to the nearest restaurant – 5km 10km 15km – don't forget 10km on a winding mountain rural road takes a lot longer than on the main road!!

38. Places to go, people to see

If you intend to rent out at some stage then you might want to consider what there is to see of interest in the area. One of the best sources of information are the travel guides which can be bought from any book shop or from the internet. Another great source of information is the official tourism website, *www.bulgariatravel.org* where you can browse by region.

39. Long or short?

How far do you want to travel from the nearest airport to your new abode? At the time of writing there are four Bulgarian airports – Sofia, the capital, Plovdiv, and on the coast – Bourgas and Varna. Don't forget though – you also have the option of flying to Istanbul in Turkey – or Bucharest in Romania – if you buy near to the border.

40. Transfer

How are you going to get from the airport to your property? If its just for you and you are visiting lots then hiring a car is an alternative option to getting a taxi – but if you are renting – most people may want to have the transfer arranged for them, so the viability of this also has to be considered.

41. Check out your surroundings

If your estate agent takes you straight to the property – be sure to check out the nearest village and surrounding area. Some villages because they are rural are obviously also very poor – but in my experience villages can be VERY different. Some are respected and clean and tidy – other look like ghost towns where there are broken windows and there is no respect for nature – rubbish is thrown into the rivers and scattered about on the roads.

42. What do you want?

There's rural and there's rural. Be clear of what type of scenery you would like to be surrounded by and make sure your estate agents is aware of this. Sounds obvious – but there are some lovely rural properties on vast open plains and there are some lovely rural properties in the mountains and there are some lovely rural properties in the green green hills! Decide what you like, refer to the maps and this may help you narrow your search and avoid wasting time looking at properties that aren't suitable.

43. Enjoy your own company

Foreigners cannot buy property in Bulgaria – to be able to do this, you have to set up a company. It's simple and easy to do but does cost – so you need to build this into your budget. You can register your limited liability company in Bulgaria with you as its sole owner and director and joint ownership is allowed too. Your estate agent can organise this for you but charges vary so check it out. At the time of writing the average seems to be between £400 and £600.

44. What's in a name?

Don't forget to think of a name for your company. You can have hours of fun at home with this bit before you go.

45. 20 Days Later...

The whole process of setting up the company takes up to 20 working days but you do not need to stay in Bulgaria for this time – if you give power of attorney to your estate agent he can act on your behalf and can organise the paperwork for you and also sign preliminary contracts and even conclude the sale for you in your absence.

46. Open an account

One of the first things to do is to open a personal Bulgarian bank account. To open a personal account costs nothing – you just need a minimum deposit – something like £10. The estate agent can do this for you – however, it is very easy to do yourself if the bank manager speaks English – however if this is not the case – then you don't stand a chance. It's much easier to get the estate agent's interpreter to go with you.

46. On the starting blocks

You need a minimum of 5000 leva to start you off (approx £2,100). This is the minimum capital amount needed by Bulgarian Law for establishing a limited liability company. It's not the cost – it just needs to be deposited in your account to show that you mean to continue business and not have a huge overdraft and take all their money out of the country. You need to deposit this amount into your bank account to enable you to make a deposit on a property and pay for the set up of the company. Any further money can then be sent over from your British bank–by–bank transfer – the cost of which is between £18 and £25.

47. A view to a kill

Viewing fees – some charge, some don't but most are refundable if you buy a property from the agent you view with. These can range from £30 per day to £100 per day – but some of the lower daily fees do not include a charge per kilometre travelled. I paid 20 eurocents per kilometre – and when you are viewing rural properties – you can get through an awful lot of kilometres.

48. Other costs for your company

A yearly cost will be incurred as you have to declare the books of the company. Obviously if you are not buying and selling and just have the one property these are zero – because your profits are zero. All you have to allow is for the cost to employ an accountant to declare the books. The cost of this at present is about £50 and you can arrange for an accountant via your estate agent if you wish.

49. Annual local taxes to be paid

Well – it certainly wont be as much as your council tax in the UK. Local taxes will be well under £100 and home and contents insurance will range from about £70 to £150 per year depending on the value of your house. In assessing your rate of tax, all sorts of things can apply – whether its an old or new property, whether it has been renovated, whether its just a holiday home and not used for a greater part of the year, whether it is in a village with a very poor infrastructure – you may be able to reduce the tax for many reasons – but remember – it will be low – so no use in worryin'

50. Services – electricity, water, waste

The cost of these is going to be low – all living costs are low. A typical heating bill for a three bedroom house will be about £100 per year – or about £10 per month. Water is a couple of pounds a month and there is a garbage charge of about £20 per year dependant upon the size of your property.

51. Capital gains tax

If you intend to resell at a later date the Bulgarian captial gains tax is currently 19.5%. This is 19.5% of the profit – ie the difference between the price you paid and the price you sell at. If you can offset any other expenses to reduce the profit your tax will be minimised. If this has been your only property and if you have owned it for more than 5 years, you will pay no taxes when selling it. For more information on tax check out *www.worldwide–tax.com* and click on Bulgaria.

52. Deposit

If you have decided on the property or properties you would like to buy and you have set up your company (if buying a house), then the first thing to do is to put a deposit on to reserve the property. Normally, an estate agent will not reserve a property without a deposit. If you want to be sure that it is not offered to anyone else, a 10% deposit is usually required. to secure the property, then the owner knows you are serious about the sale.

53. Survey

An inspection of the property will then be arranged. There are two types of survey that you can have – a visual survey where a structural engineer views the property and compiles a report. The other survey is a full structural survey and involves taking soil samples by a geologist. This would only usually be done if the property was extremely old or there was some doubt about the land on which it was built.

54. Preliminary contracts

Preliminary contracts will then be drawn up – you don't have to be present to sign the preliminary contract and can have an independent lawyer or one that works for your estate agent. You can give them power of attorney to sign the contract and take the deposit out from your bank account.

55. Final contracts

From then the final contract will be drawn up again in both Bulgarian and English.

56. Two prices – too confusing

In Bulgaria, as in many other countries there is a "tax estimation price" and a "purchase price" The TEP is for the purposes of real estate taxation and is much lower than the actual selling price. Most Bulgarian property vendors wish that the TEP is written in the title deed – so avoiding higher taxes. This is why there may be a discrepancy in the price you pay and the price that is written in the deeds. The practice is in fact illegal but still very common. Some agents insist that the real price is shown on the deeds.

57. There's someone living in my house!

Do not expect the owners to move out on the completion day. It is accepted practice that the previous owners have one month to move out of the property after the final contract date. If you wish to move in sooner, this can always be negotiated at the time and written into the contract.

58. Fees – buy and sell

If you ever sell – in Bulgaria both the buyer and the seller pay fees to estate agents (thank goodness UK agents haven't cottoned on to this!) To sell a property is usually between 2% and 5% and of course you have to pay capital gains tax, currently 19.5% between the cost of the property and the selling price. (A good reason for having the "real selling price" on the deeds when you buy rather than a lower one!)

59. Fire and tempest

The cost of house and contents insurance obviously varies depending on the value of the house. As a guide, for a property valued at about £20,000 it would cost in the region of £80–£100 per year for insurance against theft, flood and fire.

60. Lock it all up – what security do you need

For a house that is waiting to be renovated, if the property is walled on all sides, a simple padlock on the gate will be sufficient. For security on a new or renovated furnished home a more robust system is recommended.

61. It's a gas – but not underground yet

The gas system network is not yet developed in Bulgaria. Heating is mainly coal and wood. Wood burning stoves are a particularly cheap way to heat a home. There are gas central heating systems in the larger cities and there appear to be some companies that will offer to install LPG systems for you. Most central heating systems are fuelled by electricity.

62. Electricity

Most people cook on electricity. A typical bill for lighting, cooking and hot water would be about £150 per year.

63. Labour of love – and other maintenance

Labour is very inexpensive in Bulgaria. The average wage in Bulgaria is £100 per month. To employ a gardener or someone to do simple maintenance will be very low. Dry stone walling for instance you could get someone for £12 per day – yes, per DAY not per hour!

64. Driving you crazy – the prices are crazy

Annual road tax, for say a car with 2000 cc engine would be approximately £30. Insurance would be about £20 per year and an MOT cost just £8. The cost of fuel is about 50 pence per litre for petrol and lpg only 20 pence per litre. Most cars in Bulgaria are equipped with LPG systems.

65. A new car – the cheapest in Europe

Bulgaria has the cheapest brand new cars in Europe. For example a new Renault Clio cost only £4,000!

66. Chill out – with a cool pool

A pool is probably going to be the most expensive thing to maintain at a property. At the beginning of the season the pool needs to be cleaned (by local labour of course so not so expensive) and refilled – cheaper if you get it from a well than if you have a metered water supply. Two major costs for a pool are the chemicals and the electricity to run the pump and these can be, obviously depending on the size of your pool – between £10 – £25 per month during the months of June to September.

67. What's in your fruit bowl?

Different agents have differing costs – for both properties, their own fees and company set up costs. Make sure to compare the TOTAL cost of buying a property. Each agent can be different – one may have cheaper properties but high company set up costs. Another may have low company set up costs but higher property prices. It is difficult to compare apples with apples – you have to look at the whole fruit bowl!

68. I wanna be your number one!

Because of the sudden and overwhelming interest in Bulgaria, some estate agents are receiving hundreds of phone calls a day and hundreds of emails a day. They are completely overwhelmed with requests from people wanting to buy and are VERY VERY busy – so – you may NOT be their number one. Allow for this – with allocating as much time as you can for viewing – don't go for the quick trip and expect to see everything that you want – you will be disappointed. You may need more than one trip to decide exactly what you want.

69. Does the left hand know what the right hand's doin'?

If you are dealing with non–english estate agents – remember we do have some cultural differences! I don't think there is a "manyana" ethos with the Bulgarians, but I did experience a lack of commitment when it came to turning up at the time arranged. Two or three hours late was not uncommon. And I definitely had problems with the promise of "I will get back to you". They didn't. I think it was more of a problem with organisational skills and being completely overwhelmed by the number of people they have to deal with. This may well be sorted by now – but my gut feeling is that it could go on for some time. If an agent agrees to meet you at your hotel at 9am – write it down. This is not a reminder for you – but a reminder for them. Make sure they know your expectations – and get cross if they are not met – you are competing with a lot of other people out there and your time is precious.

70. Don't let them mess with your un–negotiables!

When you are trying to decide what to view – or explaining what you would like to your estate agent – its useful to have your "top three". These are your top three requirements that you are NOT prepared to negotiate on. For example – if you definitely definitely definitely want a property with a view of the mountains – or a property that is not more than 10km from civilisation – then make sure you include these in your top three un–negotiables. There is so much to see you can very easily waste a lot of time (and money) being persuaded to view lots of properties that are very very nice – but are just not what you really really wanted.

71. Be flexible with your negotiables!

Be specific with your top three – but be flexible with your other requirements. You may think you want a property with at least 1000m² of land, but when you see a property that has fantastic views, is in a beautiful village, is in excellent condition but only has 800m2 of land instead of your required 1000m2 – are you really THAT bothered? Are you really going to pass on a 'bargain of a beaut' because it has a few square meters of soil less than you wanted? Be specific – but flexible !

72. So what are you looking for?

When an agent asks you this question – and you have to describe what kind of property you are looking for – think about the detail. So you want a view? Is this a view of the mountains, or are you happy with a view overlooking the town? So you want land? Do you want undulating hills just to look at or do you want flat land to do something with it? Think about the specifics and write a list.

73. Stay connected – take a phone

You need to be able to chase your agents – they have many customers and are being pulled in a million and one different directions. YOU need to be able to contact THEM to keep on top of any progress or arrange more viewings.

74. Service with a smile

When choosing an agent – think about how you are being treated – do they get back to you when they promise, do they keep you informed, do they have your best interests at heart – or are you chasing them the whole time, being let down on appointments and generally being given excuse after excuse for very simple mistakes? If it's like that when you are there – what's the service going to be like when you get back home?

75. To be on the safe side...

Tell them your Dad is a lawyer.

76. Never refuse a bag of plums

Some owners will want to come with you on your viewing – HOWEVER they may not be available at the exact moment you want to view! Sounds obvious – but don't assume that you will be able to see all your dream homes on the same day. Allow plenty of time to arrange viewings – the more the better. Each owner may offer you something from his property to entice you to buy – this can range from a bag of plums or an entire antique china dinner service.

77. What the best–dressed property viewer is wearing this year

The Bulgarians are very fashion conscious – so be sure you are dressed correctly. THIS MEANS IT DOESN'T MATTER HOW HOT IT IS – MAKE SURE YOU WEAR LONG TROUSERS. This has in fact, got nothing to do with fashion and everything to do with creepy crawly things in the long grass. With many properties you will have to trail through a veritable jungle of long grass, sometimes up to your waist, often up to your armpits. Keep the open toed sandals and flip flops for the rest and relaxation days.

78. Forget your toothbrush by all means –
but be sure to pack your imagination

When you look at properties at the lower end of the market you are REALLY going to need that imagination – and lots of it. When the toilet is in a wooden hut at the end of the garden, the rooms are small and dark and you are wondering how on earth these people keep warm in the winter – this is when you have to "look beyond what the eye can see" and dream about how it COULD look given a good team of inexpensive Bulgarian builders.

79. Does your memory serve you well?

Take a camera, even better take a digital camera, even better take a video camera. Take pics of every property you see from every angle. Even take pictures of the local village and surroundings. If you have digital or video then you can look at these in the evening in your hotel. When you are so punch drunk because you have seen so many properties in such a short time, they will be useful reminder. If you don't make a decision on buying while you are in Bulgaria, you will find the photos very useful when you return to the UK.

80. What do you want, do you really really want?

Keep asking yourself this question. At the beginning of the day and at the end of the day and all through the day. Does this property give me what I really want? Keep doing this and you will be fine. If you don't ask yourself this question frequently, you can very easily buy something that you don't want. Obvious – but easier to do than you think.

81. Where's the sun gone?

Check out the time when you are at the property. You may be planning to be out in the sun all day on your terrace – but check out the position of the sun and any surrounding buildings or hills. It could be that you will only get the sun on your fantastic terrace for half an hour.

82. Is it a ghost town?

If you are taken straight to the property – remember to check out the village. Villages vary enormously – some are quaint and well kept – others look like ghost towns. Be sure you take a drive around the immediate surrounding area to check it out and get your bearings.

83. Quirky reminders

Take the printed details of the property with you if possible. If not, write down on a piece of paper: the name of the village, the price of the property, a short description or the points that stand out for you any quirky things to remind you which property it is!

If you see a few properties in the same day – or even spread out over the week you will not remember which is which. You tend to get "punch drunk" and confused very very quickly. No matter what else you do – write these little reminders down as you go. One property I viewed, I just could not, for the life of me, bring to mind – then I looked at my notes and it said, "Next door neighbour was holding a newborn kitten". It suddenly all came flooding back!

84. The big freeze

If you are viewing in the summer – boy is it different in the winter! If you want to be able to visit your rural retreat in the winter as well – be sure it's in a place where you can get proper access to your property. You just won't get through on many roads to rural properties during the winter.

85. Wealth Warning!

When you see something you like and it fits your requirements – STOP. There's a tendancy to think that there will be something else better round the corner that you might miss. However, I truly believe you can get "hooked" on viewing – it's definitely addictive and should carry a government health (or wealth) warning. You can waste a lot of time, and more importantly money, on viewing with the expectation that you might find something better tomorrow. If it satisfies your top three 'un–negotiables' and feels right – buy it and stop viewing.

86. Black tie

Not what to wear while you are viewing necessarily, but don't be surprised if you view a property and there is a huge piece of black material pinned to the front door in the shape of a bow. It is usually accompanied by an A4 sheet of paper and sometimes a photo of the owner giving details of his or her life and who has since departed this earth. Show respect if you are viewing with the previous owner's relative – although one house I viewed he insisted that I took anything I wanted from inside the house with me. Somehow it didn't feel quite right.

87. The Biggest Tip of All!

TAKE THIS BOOK WITH YOU

GEMS

Just a few little gems to make you smile. They are quoted straight from estate agents' property details. They seem to like their sales copy to rhyme on occasions. Presumably these were meant to tempt you to buy?

"Something everyone adores – to have a toilet indoors"

"In the village at the end – just next door to your best friend"

"The region is full of exotic places – forests, rocky slopes
and meadows – which give you a very special sensation."

"Have you ever dreamed of a device to prepare smoked food?"

"There is 1000 square meters of garden – one could
have one's own fresh fruit to taste and waste."

"The garden is perfect for trying the charm of your own flowers"

"This looks unreal. But it is"

"All refrigerators, television sets and hunters
trophies are included in the price"

"All kinds of fruit and vegetables are grown there –
like a small farm – away from dirty plants."

"This house is really very lonely, away from other houses"

"Here you can hang a kind of dried meat garnished
with hunting stories and legends!"

71

WEBSITES TO VISIT

ESTATE AGENTS

www.balkanskichalet.com
www.balkanvillas.com
www.barrasfordandbird.co.uk
www.bg–aa.com *
www.bulgariancoastalproperties.com
www.bulgariandreams.com
www.bulgarianproperties.com
www.bulgariaplus.com
www.easybg.com
www.easyrealty–bulgaria.com
www.edendevelopments.co.uk
www.homes–bg.com
www.hotbulgariaproperties.com
www.stara–planina.com *

* denotes agents who have been particularly helpful to me.

BULGARIAN FORUMS

www.britsinbulgaria.com
www.mybulgaria.info

GENERAL INFORMATION AND TRAVEL

www.air.bg

www.beachbulgaria.com

www.bgmaps.com

www.btibulgaria.com

www.bulgariancoast.com

www.bulgarianembassy.org.uk

www.bulgaria–property.org

www.bulgariaski.com

www.bulgariatravel.org

www.rentacarbulgaria.com

www.worldwide–tax.com

ABOUT THE AUTHOR

Joanna Losack dreamed of owning a house in the mountains, so that she and her two children could have fun 'getting back to nature' and experiencing a slower pace of life. Joanna discovered Bulgaria and after a year of researching property on the internet, experienced the 'adventure of a lifetime' with her two young boys on their first visit to Bulgaria. Driving round the rural villages, exploring the countryside, and tracking down properties with the help of local estate agents and the local people, she was captivated by the Bulgarian welcome. She returned to the UK having bought her mountain house for just £3,500 which doubled in value over 4 months. Joanna has now built up a portfolio of properties to rent out, so that others too, may experience the stunning scenery, clean fresh air, delicious food and warm welcome from the local Bulgarians.

Jo first trained as a journalist in London at the age of 22. Her articles on Bulgaria have been published in property magazines and guides both in the UK and abroad. After spending ten years in advertising and marketing, Jo completely changed career direction and spent the next ten years working with youngsters who had problems attending school.

At the age of 40, Jo discovered her true passion in life and set up her own life coaching company, The Magic of Coaching, (*www.themagicofcoaching.com*) so that she could motivate, support and empower other people to enable them to take action to achieve their dreams.

Joanna is currently working on her next book, *Renovating Property In Bulgaria.*

Email: joanna@fastforward1.freeserve.co.uk
www.themagicofbulgaria.com
www.themagicofcoaching.com

Printed in the United Kingdom
by Lightning Source UK Ltd.
105937UKS00001B/79-96